"I LOVE HER, BUT..."

"… she leaves the seat down."

—MARK, VAIL, CO

"I LOVE HER, BUT…"

BY ROBERT LLEWELLYN JONES

WORKMAN PUBLISHING • NEW YORK

Library of Congress Cataloging-in-Publication Data

I love her, but…—/Merry Bloch Jones and Robert Llewellyn Jones.
p. cm.—ISBN 0-7611-0473-9
1. Wives—Quotations, maxims, etc. 2. Wives—Humor.
I. Jones, Robert Llewellyn. II. Title. III. Title: Things women do
that drive their husbands crazy

PN6084.W55J65   1996   306.872—dc20   96-584   CIP

*Workman books are available at special discounts
when purchased in bulk for premiums and sales
promotions as well as for fund-raising or
educational use. Special editions or book excerpts can
also be created to specification. For details,
contact the Special Sales Director at the address below.*

Workman Publishing Company, Inc.
708 Broadway, New York, NY 10003-9555

Manufactured in the United States of America
First Printing January 1996

10 9 8 7 6 5 4 3 2 1

to Baille and Neely
and the men they'll drive crazy

ACKNOWLEDGMENTS

Thanks to Connie Clausen, Lynn Brunelle, all the husbands who were candid and the wives who took it in stride. Most of all, thanks to my wife, Merry Bloch Jones, without whom this book could never have been written.

INTRODUCTION

Mr. Jones was not amused. In fact he was baffled. Indignant. Maybe even a little wounded. "What's so funny?" he asked. He'd just finished reading Mrs. Jones' book, "*I Love Him, But…*", which lists hundreds of things men do that make their wives crazy. "Women are just as bad," he claimed. "Probably worse."

"Don't be ridiculous," Mrs. Jones answered. "There's no comparison."

"Ask any man. Any married man will tell you. Women are much more difficult to live with than men."

"Says you."

"Says anybody who has a clue about what married men put up with."

"Bet?"

"Bet."

And so, they were on. Their goal: to determine which gender is harder to live with. They already knew how hard men are to live with; women had already expressed their views in *"I Love Him, But…"* The task remained to ask men what, if anything, their wives do that drives them crazy.

"I Love Her, But…" is the result. It gives equal time to the hairier sex. The requirements were that the men interviewed be happily married, wed for at least six years and currently living with their spouses.

Mr. & Mrs. Jones collected answers from over two hundred husbands all over the United States. Some were family, friends or friends of friends; others were randomly encountered on e-mail or at convention halls, ball games, health spas, trains, service stations, planes, country clubs, parties, markets, national parks, barbershops and bowling alleys in fifty states.

The men ranged in age from twenty-six to eighty-two, and represented all races, many religions and a wide variety of professions, from doctors to lawyers to truckers and taxi drivers.

Although some men were eager to talk, the majority required substantial prodding before listing their peeves. However, whether squirming or smiling, intimating or imitating, each aired his wife-related gripes with loving good humor. Once started, in fact, a number got carried away. "Somebody stop me," one man begged. "You could do a whole book on my wife alone."

Even the most devoted husbands confessed that the adorable, irresistible, captivating loves of their lives at times drove them wall-climbingly, teeth-grindingly nuts. Their compiled comments present a candid and unique view of wives and marriage, as seen through the eyes of the wedded American male. The book tells women how their spouses perceive them, reassures men that they do not suffer alone and increases understanding, or at least acceptance, between the sexes.

Further, by defining exactly what married men have to put up with, the book settles the bet between the Joneses.

"See! I win," gloats Mr. Jones.

"Based on what?" asks Mrs. Jones.

"Based on all these husbands' comments, of course. They prove beyond the shadow of a doubt that women are more difficult to live with than men."

"No way. They prove exactly the opposite. If you actually compared them to the women's comments, you'd see that I've won. But, as usual, despite all the evidence to the contrary, you're convinced that you're right."

"Really? And I suppose you're completely objective?"

"Of course. If and when I'm wrong, I'll admit it."

Mr. Jones shakes his head. "You're just amazing."

"Thanks, dear," Mrs. Jones agrees. "Anyway, I'm glad it's finally settled. Aren't you?" She snuggles up beside him.

"Yes, dear. Of course, dear." His arm slides comfortably around her. "Whatever you say."

"I LOVE HER, BUT..."

"...she has an uncanny way of standing between me and the television screen. Bases loaded, two strikes, three balls. The crowd goes wild, the pitch flies, and all I can see is her butt."

—HOWARD, DODGE CITY, KS

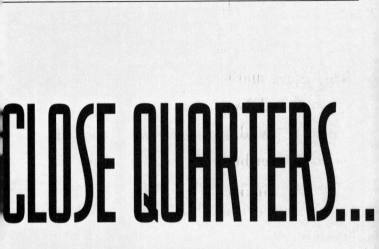

CLOSE QUARTERS...

FOR BETTER OR WORSE

Soon after the honeymoon, marriage begins to usurp a man's time and turf. Nothing, anymore, can guarantee him exclusive territory or personal space. His wife empties his pockets, reorganizes his bureau, throws out his comfy old sweaters, sorts his mail. The scents of hairspray and nail polish remover waft through his home; his clothes are relegated to the smaller half of the closet; the beer he tries to keep in the refrigerator loses ground to diet soda.

Whether the problems are diet, decor or division of chores, however, sharing space inevitably requires a balance of power. "My wife," one husband explains, "believes that a man's home is his wife's castle. We have no problems about living together, as long as I obey."

"...she never fills the gas tank. Every other week, she runs out of gas. She thinks the local gas station runs a delivery service."

—BOB, GLENVIEW, IL

"...she has the TV on all the time. Doesn't know what's on, isn't watching, just wants it on. Gets mad if I turn it off."

—FRANK, DETROIT, MI

"...she can't let me read the paper in peace. At breakfast, she grabs the section she wants. Never mind that I might be reading it at the time."

—STEPHEN, WILLOUGHBY, OH

"...she was furious when I got up early once and made her breakfast. Called me controlling. How dare I decide that she would eat breakfast, let alone what she'd have?"

—TED, WEXFORD, PA

"...when she sneezes, the roof shakes. And she never sneezes only once. It's always four times, in succession. But sometimes she'll give three big ATCHOOs, and then you sit, waiting. You know the fourth one's coming; you just don't know exactly when."

—MILES, SHREVEPORT, LA

"...she's always cold. Turns on the heat in the summer. Likes it sweltering."

—BILL, ALLENTOWN, PA

"...she's always late. Mornings are always a last-minute rush, a contest for the shower, a battle for the sink, a growled goodbye."

—GEORGE, FORESTVILLE, MD

"I LOVE HER, BUT..."

"...she must not and will not be interrupted. If she's on the phone, dressing, making lists, thinking. I can't interrupt. Not even for a quick kiss goodbye in the morning; I have to wait until she's done with her shower. If a band of barbarians attacked while she was doing her hair, they'd have to wait, too."

—MILTON, BOCA RATON, FL

"...she uses the term 'we' all the time. 'We' like such-and-such. 'We' think so-and-so. As if we're one being, one brain, one opinion. One mouth."

—RICK, MEDFORD, NJ

"...she tidies up by throwing the newspaper out before I've even had a chance to read it."

—BRENDAN, KENILWORTH, IL

"...she'll make a comment that seems to be from Mars, a complete non sequitur. But then I realize she's continuing some discussion we had days or weeks ago. To her, conversations are continuous and interwoven. They can get interrupted by five minutes or five years, but she can pick them up anytime, wherever she left off."

—VICTOR, DES PLAINES, IL

"...she turns to me and, in all seriousness, asks: 'What was I just going to say?'"

—LEON, WASHINGTON, DC

"...she never says what she means. To her, words are irrelevant. Interchangeable. She'll tell me to put the juice in the garage instead of the refrigerator, or to turn off the water when she means the oven, or to turn when she means go straight. And she expects me to know what she means. What worries me is that, usually, I do."

—LARRY, ATLANTA, GA

"...whenever I express an opinion, she says, 'Tsk. Oh, please.' Whenever I tell a joke, she says, 'Tsk. Oh, please.' Whenever I grab her butt, she says, 'Tsk. Oh, please.'"

—JACK, JACKSON, MI

"...what's mine is hers. I buy her negligees; she sleeps in my T-shirts. When she's cold, she wears my wool socks to bed, never her own. She steals my half-used razors; new ones are too sharp. She even wears my boxers. I'm tempted to switch to briefs just to see what she'd do."

—DAVE, MARTHA'S VINEYARD, MA

"I LOVE HER, BUT..."

"...she calls my office forty times a day. Over everything. I get interrupted so she can tell me what bills came in the mail. Or what the weather's going to be at rush hour—I get daily reports on the weather. 'Listen, Sid— It's gonna rain later.'"

—SIDNEY, CHEVY CHASE, MD

"...she borrows my clothes.

Permanently."

—MARK, EVANSTON, IL

"...she sniffs clothes before she puts them in the wash. Like, why? I mean, if today's socks or underwear don't smell, does she think we should wear them again tomorrow?"

—TOM, ST. CLOUD, MN

"...her jewelry's all over the house. I find earrings in the shower. In bed. On the kitchen counter. On the stove. Then she's always late, panicked, because she can't find them. She's sure we've been robbed."

—EVAN, NORTH PLATTE, NE

"...I'm convinced that she sprays my closet and the sheets with her perfume. Everything I own smells like flowers."

—GEOFFREY, NEW MEADOWS, IA

"...the woman has every color nail polish ever manufactured. She has special racks to hold them, can see a hundred bottles all at once. But she arranges them by gradations of color, so every new bottle means hours of rearranging. Every time she shops, she buys more. I could paint the house with them."

—HANK, PHOENIX, AZ

"...she likes perfume—a lot.
You can tell she's home with
your eyes closed."

—RUSS, BUFFALO, NY

"... her theory of housekeeping is, 'Why clean? Move.'"

—DON, HALF MOON BAY, CA

"...whatever I do around the house, she redoes. Run the vacuum. Load the dishwasher. Whatever. Then she tells me that I never do anything."

—KEVIN, CHICAGO, IL

"...she grunts while she cleans. Dusting a shelf, polishing a table, she goes, 'Uh. Ungh. Umph.' I offer to do it just to stop the noise."

—DYLAN, WILMINGTON, DE

"...she has allergies. I find wadded-up tissues, still wet, all over the place. I sit on them. I step on them. I find them under the covers, in bed."

—BRYAN, AMARILLO, TX

"...she controls the paper towels, allots a certain number for each task. No more. And no less."

—WALTER, BETHESDA, MD

"...she makes lists. Things to buy. Things to do. People to call. If it's not on the list, it doesn't get done. Once, to be funny, I put 'sex' on the list. Mistake. Now it has to be on the list or it doesn't get done."

—NICK, WHEELING, WV

"...everything has to be sterile. She scrubbed the cage with ammonia and accidentally killed the guinea pig."

—FRANK, OLYMPIA, WA

"...she leaves these symbolic messages for me to interpret. Let's say she found some of my clothes on the floor. She'd never carry them to the laundry. Instead, she'd pick them up and drop them on my pillow. Say I were to leave a coffee mug in the john. Instead of taking it to the kitchen, she'd put my razor, comb and toothbrush in it. If I forget my robe and she finds it by the shower, she won't simply hang it in the closet. She'll slide it across the floor and leave it on my side of the bathroom."

—DARREN, CINCINNATI, OH

"...she's always beginning one project and dropping it for another. We have half-finished paintings, pottery, afghans, wallpapering, novels and needle points all over the place. The other day she said something about how much fun it would be to build a sailboat!"

—FRED, LOS ANGELES, CA

"... when she gets an idea in her head, there's no stopping her. And no rest for anyone until it's done. It's not so bad when the idea is to bake cookies, or even to go on vacation. But when it's to build a new house, or to get pregnant, things get pretty intense."

—JIM, MINNEAPOLIS, MN

"...she's a brilliant woman with a master's degree, well-read, cultured, but she can never find her keys. I mean never."

—MICHAEL, AUSTIN, TX

"...she doesn't like technology, so we were the last family in the country to get a color television. I bought her a microwave. She uses it to store bread. The computer I gave her two years ago is still in its box, unopened."

—BRYAN, ST. PAUL, MN

"...there are certain jobs, for all her liberation, that she will not do. She doesn't refuse to do them; it simply never occurs to her that she might actually change a light bulb. Or empty the trash compactor. If she sees an insect, she traps it under a glass until I get home."

—TOM, WASHINGTON, DC

"I LOVE HER, BUT..."

"...our house is her museum. You can't walk on the white carpets, can't put your cup on the coffee table, can't leave water marks on formica counters. You can breathe, but not near the mirrors."

—ABE, WAIMEA, HI

"... she saves all the 'good stuff'—the booze, china, wine, linens. I don't have a clue what she's saving it for. We've been married for fourteen years and haven't taken most of our wedding gifts out of the boxes."

—WILLIAM, HARRISBURG, PA

"...my wife never throws out anything. She's got plastic containers full of spare buttons and safety pins, boxes full of plastic containers and paper bags. She has drawers filled with old toothbrushes, sponges. A drawer for single socks. Our kids are in high school. She still has their diapers."

—LEW, FRAMINGHAM, MA

"...she never relaxes. Getting the laundry done is more important than having a glass of wine. She can't sleep if there are dishes in the sink."

—PHILIP, BETHESDA, MD

"...she never empties the dishwasher. She uses it as a cabinet."

—AUSTIN, AMHERST, MA

"I LOVE HER, BUT..."

"...she clears the table while you're still eating, gathers up the newspaper while you're reading it, has your clothes in the washer before they hit the floor."

—DARNELL, JACKSON, WY

"...she cleans our house before the cleaning help arrives. She doesn't want them to see a mess."

—ROBERT, WILMINGTON, DE

"...when she's upset, she cleans. I know there's trouble if I come home and find the house immaculate. Or if I wake up and hear the vacuum in the middle of the night."

—AL, DALLAS, TX

"...she cleans before leaving the house. The kids and I are in the car, ready to go. That's when she starts making the beds, throwing out the trash, doing the dishes. She says she doesn't want to come home to a mess."

—JOE, BANGOR, ME

"...she loads the dish-washer while I'm unloading clean dishes. Then she gets mad at me for putting dirty dishes away."

—MARK, EVANSTON, IL

lways on a diet.
o out to eat, she
all salad. And then
my plate."

N

"... if I'm doing the dishes, she gets between me and the sink and does them, too. If I'm cooking, she gets between me and the stove, stirs, tastes, adds pepper. If I'm in the shower, she steps in under the hot water. The only place she doesn't step in front of me is at the toilet."

—MARVIN, BROOKLYN, NY

"...she's carnivorous. Gnaws the bones afterwards. You don't want to get between her and a pork chop."

—TODD, CINCINNATI, OH

"...if you
in your ha
thing, not
of milk c
yogurt or
for, say,
after she
all back

—JON, N

"...she's a
When we g
orders a sn
she eats off

—ROB, NASHVILLE, T

"...everything's rare. Fine, if it's steak, but chicken? Chocolate cake?"

—TED, MILWAUKEE, WI

"...she's always dieting and she resents everyone who isn't. She'll sit with her bowl of cottage cheese and glare at me while I eat."

—DEREK, AUGUSTA, GA

"...no matter what, *I* have to go on *her* diets!"

—SAM, BROOKLYN, NY

"...she'll order an ice cream float in a diet soda. Or she'll have pecan pie with whipped cream and put artificial sweetener in her coffee."

—ART, ESCONDIDO, CA

"...my wife thinks everyone should be a vegetarian. During meals, she asks people how they can eat dead cows, or if they know that their pork chops were once smarter than their dogs."

—MILES, SHREVEPORT, LA

"...she always fussing with me. No matter where we are or who's around. I get this appraising squint and unless I move quickly, she starts picking stuff off my jacket or rearranging my hair. Right in public! Or she'll lick her finger and smooth my eyebrows."

— GARRETT, FORT LAUDERDALE, FL

"... she picks out my clothes. Tells me which shirt and pants to wear, which socks. I have a lot of stuff she won't let me wear, even around the house."

— BLAIR, BLOOMINGTON, IN

"...she leaves notes taped to the inside of the toilet seat. Reminding me that we have dinner plans. Or to mail a letter. Or to wipe the rim with lysol when I'm done."

—DARREN, CINCINNATI, OH

TALES OF THE HEAD

All across America, husbands struggle through occupied female territory just to get to the john. They begin their days dodging dripping panty hose to get to the shower, uprooting clumps of long hair to unclog the drain and clearing cosmetics off the sink to get a shave.

Nonetheless, many are philosophical about power politics in their marital baths. Whether they get ousted, crowded or brushed, they see it as a place where their most private issues come to a head, their most vulnerable sides get exposed. Before medicine cabinets and mirrors, amid blow dryers and bubbles, with close shaves and clean sweeps, bathroom interactions flush out the basics, bringing couples together, face to face and cheek to cheek.

"...the bathtub is her personal spa. She has an inflatable pillow, a floating tray. She stays in there for hours with her bubbles, books and bonbons."

—RAY, ATLANTA, GA

"... my wife gets into the shower with me. She adjusts the temperature to suit her. Then she complains that I'm splashing water in her eyes."

—MARC, BALTIMORE, MD

"...she dries her hair with my towel. It's always damp."

—GREG, DENVER, CO

"...she darts ahead of me, races to get to the toilet first. Tells me she's quicker, that I take too long."

—SID, MORTON GROVE, IL

"...she insists that men mess the floor around the toilet. She leaves a sponge and a can of toilet cleaner there, and wants me to scrub the bowl whenever I take a leak."

—LEROY, CARMEL, CA

"...we have an ongoing toilet paper war. She wants the loose end out; I want it the right way—toward the wall."

—DAVE, DULUTH, MN

"...if I get a blackhead, she wants to squeeze it. She insists on trimming my nose and ear hairs, chases me around snapping a scissors."

—BOB, GLENVIEW, IL

"...we have to have two sinks in the bathroom. She keeps hers immaculate just to demonstrate how filthy mine is. She warns people, before they go in, not to look at mine."

—PETER, LARCHMONT, NEW YORK

"...after she takes a shower, she never puts on clothes. She's basically a nudist. Does the housework in the altogether. It's gotten so I don't even notice. And she forgets, too. The pizza man loves to come to our house."

—LEWIS, MIAMI, FL

"...her nails are so long that if she ever made a sudden fist, she'd slash her wrists."

—VINCE, PITTSBURGH, PA

"...she spends hours picking the dry skin off her feet."

—CRAIG, DETROIT, MI

"...she won't let anyone see her feet. She's convinced they're ugly. I tell her that everybody's feet are ugly. She says, 'What difference does that make?'"

—HERB, ST. LOUIS, MO

"…she's always with the tweezers. Leaning into a magnifying mirror and plucking at something."

—BERNIE, SACRAMENTO, CA

"...she has tattoos. Nobody knows this but me, my wife and the tattoo artist, if you know what I mean."

—SETH, NEW YORK, NY

"... every so often, *boom:* she's a brunette. Or I come home to a redhead. Actually, I have no idea what her natural color is."

—CARY, SEATTLE, WA

"...she spends entire evenings brushing her hair. She's very proud of it. She calls it 'virgin hair.'"

—CHRIS, RICHMOND, VA

"... she spends lots of time and money painting herself with stuff that makes her look like she's not wearing makeup."

—ROGER, KING OF PRUSSIA, PA

"...she's obsessed with 'thigh flab.' She measures her thighs with a tape."

—ARI, NEW YORK, NY

"...she doesn't wear underwear. Ever."

—PAUL, DALLAS, TX

"…her eyelashes are caked with so much mascara that they'd crack if you touched them. She wakes up with matching shiners. If she cries, she looks like someone poured an ink bottle over her head."

—ROY, BOULDER, CO

"...she'll brush her teeth but she won't go to the dentist. She says she's not afraid of the pain, she just doesn't want to put herself in the hands of any fellow who'd choose to be a dentist."

—TERENCE, GARY, IN

"...she clicks her dentures. When she bothers to wear them."

—GABE, ST. LOUIS, MO

"...she gets herself waxed. Then all she can talk about is the silky texture of her legs and thighs. She caresses herself and runs her hands over her body. This goes on for days."

—PAUL, SAN ANTONIO, TX

"...there's not much mystery. She points out her varicose veins, gray hair, facial hairs, pimples, ingrown toenails, corns, hemorrhoids."

—NED, GARY, IN

"...she's stopped shaving her legs. She says that now people will know she's a natural blonde."

—NED, TUCSON, AZ

"... she's phobic about her physical condition. Lives in mortal fear of cancer. High blood pressure. And zits."

—NED, FORT WASHINGTON, PA

"...no matter what she's doing, she exercises. She jogs in place in the bathroom while she brushes her teeth, does leg lifts in the tub, stretches when she towels off. The woman never sits still."

—ROGER, MEMPHIS, TN

"...she wears color-coded underpants. Red means she's hot. Pastels and flower patterns indicate that she wants to be babied. White means cool it; she's a virgin again. Black, forget it."

—DON, RICHMOND, VA

"...all that concerns her in this world is water retention. She weighs herself three times a day."

—ELIAS, BALTIMORE, MD

"...she truly believes that her period is a worthy subject for conversation. I mean, that people should know whether it's regular, or heavy, or if she has cramps."

—JOEL, NEW YORK, NY

"...for her birthday, I gave her a gift certificate for twenty four hours as her sex slave. She laughed. Told me I was 'sweet.'"

—GREGORY, BROOKLINE, MA

THE BEDROOM...

DISCRETION AND VALOR

Men are often reluctant to uncover the details of their marriage beds. They blush, grin, laugh, remain mum, roll their eyes, shake their heads, bounce their knees, look to the ceiling for acceptable replies. What they finally come up with is, at first, evasive and polite; the truth, for a while, stays safely undercover.

Once they set to it, though, men recount pillow thefts, blanket wars, snooze alarms, and window-rattling snores. Some see the bedroom as the stage on which marital dramas of romance, rage, coupling and scuffling are played out; others see it as a snug haven where nothing but inhibition is taboo. No matter how it's decorated or what they wear there, however, most agree that the bedroom bares the naked truth about their spouses, their marriages and themselves.

"...she takes her half of the bed out of the middle."

—ROBIN, GLADWYNE, PA

"...she can't fall asleep because she worries. So she tells me what's worrying her, feels unburdened and falls asleep. Then I stay up worrying."

—TOM, SOMERSET, NJ

"...she wakes me up at night to tell me her dreams."

—LEW, CONCORD, NH

"...she always waits till we're in bed to discuss topics like our retirement plan. And then she gets mad if I fall asleep."

—LOWELL, CHICAGO, IL

"I LOVE HER, BUT..."

"...she obsesses. I'm tired, dozing off. Every thirty seconds, she jabs me. 'Larry, do you think I'll get that new account?...Why do you think so?... That's no reason...You're not listening to me... You're just saying that so I'll be quiet; you don't really think that...' Finally, I go through it with her point by carefully explained point and begin to doze off again, and I hear, 'Larry, do you really think I'll get the account?'"

—LARRY, ATLANTA, GA

"...she rearranges me when I sleep. Turns my head, covers me, uncovers me. Pushes me onto my side."

—MIKE, BALTIMORE, MD

"...when she has cramps, nothing helps but the pressure of my butt against her belly. She wants me to sleep on my side so she can lean her stomach on it. After a while, though, I get numb. I lose feeling in half of my body. But if I try to turn over, all hell breaks loose."

—MORT, SANTE FE, NM

"...every day at three o'clock exactly, no exceptions, she must take her nap. Our lives revolve around her naptime."

—BRUCE, BRIDGEWATER, NJ

"...she kicks me if I snore."

—DIRK, SYRACUSE, NY

"...she snacks in bed. I sleep on the crumbs."

—CARY, SEATTLE, WA

"...she can't sleep without this threadbare, frayed gray rag. Her 'bankie,' from when she was a baby."

—NORM, SKOKIE, IL

"...have you ever seen a woman with green crust and slime smeared over her face, dark holes for her nostrils? Do you think you'd be able to sleep at night, knowing that creature is next to you?"

—ARTHUR, CEDAR CITY, UT

"...she's always cold. When I'm dozing off, freezing feet slither between my thighs, icy fingers under my arms. She climbs all over me to keep warm. And then she complains if I sweat."

—DAN, TERRA HAUTE, IN

"...I kick the blankets off; she pulls them up. I try to push them down again; she tugs to hold them on. If *she's* cold, *I* have to have covers."

—TRENT, NEWARK, DE

"…she never gets out of bed on her side. She climbs over me to get out because my side's closer to the bathroom."

—JOEL, NEW YORK, NY

"I LOVE HER, BUT…"

"…if I'm sick and want to stay in bed, I'm a wimp. Like all men, I fall apart at a sniffle. She gives me the line about how it's a good thing 'men don't have to have babies. The human race would be extinct.'"

—DICK, WINNETKA, IL

"...she insists that the dogs sleep with us. If we make love, they sit and watch, panting and waiting for us to finish so they can jump back in bed."

—STAN, ITHACA, NY

"...her cat sleeps on my pillow. Right on my head. If I push him off, he comes back. If I lock him out of the room, she sulks and tells me I'm selfish and cruel."

—PRESTON, SILVER LAKE, OR

"...she'll wake me up at any hour of the night to have sex. This sounds great, I know. But, believe me, it's tiring."

—JACK, LOS ANGELES, CA

"...my wife's allergic to everything. Her nose is chronically stuffed. If I kissed her on the mouth, she'd suffocate."

—BRYAN, TOLEDO, OH

"...she shaves the hairs off her arms."

—ELLIOT, FORT WAYNE, IN

"...she can't stand to have anybody breathe on her face. Sometimes she puts a pillow between our heads while we make love."

—ALAN, TUSCALOOSA, AL

"...she has a huge sexual appetite. The minute I start to relax, she's after me."

—ENZO, PHILADELPHIA, PA

"... she never tells me that she wants to make love. She lowers her chin, stares at me and blinks. And keeps on blinking."

—LEN, TAMPA, FL

"...when she wants sex, she talks baby talk and pouts."

—RICK, TACOMA, WA

"...I can tell what's on her mind—if she feels guilty about something, or wants something from me—by how she acts in bed. She has no idea how transparent she is, not a clue."

—EVERETT, LITTLE ROCK, AR

"...after sex, I mean the second after, she continues from where she left off. Her eyes open and before you can *breathe*, you hear, '... and, oh yeah, I have to defrost the chicken, and your mother wants you to pick up her dry cleaning...'"

—JIMMY, FORT LAUDERDALE, FL

"...she likes sex one way. No variations. If I try anything else, she gets annoyed and tells me to get 'on with it.'"

—ROGER, RICHMOND, VA

"...she talks to 'Mr. Johnson,' like he's a separate person with a mind and personality all his own."

—MANNY, WALLA WALLA, WA

"...she thinks it's 'our' penis. To play with or do with whenever or whatever she wants. She hangs on to it while she sleeps, like it's a lifeline."

—BRAD, NEW HAVEN, CT

"...she wants me to be a caveman in bed."

—ALEX, ATLANTA, GA

"...she chats during sex. Tells me about her day. The kids. Whatever drifts through her mind."

—STEVE, CINCINNATI, OH

"...we never have time to make love. We have four kids. The oldest is six. There's always at least one in our bed. I figure we'll have an opportunity again in, maybe, six years; five, if we're lucky."

—BRENDAN, PORTLAND, OR

"...in bed I'm her high school teacher, captain of the football team, her boss, the bad boy, a waiter, a lifeguard, a telephone repairman, a cop. Once in a while I'd like to be me."

—NEIL, ORLANDO, FL

"I LOVE HER, BUT..."

"...she prefers to have sex in public places."

—MATT, BRAINTREE, MA

"...she can never just let the phone ring. No matter what we're doing, she answers the phone on the second ring. She'll talk with her mother, right while we're in the act."

—MITCH, WASHINGTON, DC

"...She reads those romance novels, one after another. They get her steamed; she literally attacks me."

—LOU, BROOKHAVEN, PA

"...after fifty-two years of marriage, our sex life, as you might expect, isn't what it used to be. We're down to just once, maybe twice a week."

—ABE, NEW YORK, NY

"...she talks in food. Her dad's a peach, her sister's husband is a clam. Depending on her mood, I'm either dead meat or prime steak. Our kids are chickens, pumpkins, cookies, cupcakes."

—TREVOR, TALLAHASSEE, FL

SHE'S GOT WHAT IT TAKES

In describing their wives' most bothersome characteristics, many men present variations of the age-old comic quip: "She's a giving person. She's always giving grief, giving opinions, giving hell…"

Even modern, gender-unbiased husbands complain that their spouses nag, jabber, change moods unpredictably, think irrationally or set unfathomable priorities. Furthermore, their wives don't get their jokes, and they disapprove of everything from their friends to their ties.

No matter how oppressive their wives' quirks are, however, most men tolerate them, accepting what they can neither comprehend nor control. Annoyed, amused, frustrated or flabbergasted, some attribute their wives' behaviors to fluctuating hormones; others resignedly relegate them to that enigmatic, inexplicable realm reserved for the unsolvable mysteries of the "opposite" sex.

"...she wakes up singing some awful tune, then I can't get it out of my head for the rest of the day."

—TOM, SIOUX CITY, IA

"...nothing's wrong with her.
She's perfect. Has no faults at all.
She believes this, too."

—STU, CAMBRIDGE, MA

"...she always knows what I'm thinking. Finishes my sentences. Says what I'm going to say before I can form the words. Addresses my thoughts. Like, she'll say, 'You've had enough,' before I've reached for my second piece of pie. Or she'll ask, 'How's the new girl in the office working out?' I can't have any secrets, can't get away with anything."

—LEON, RED CLOUD, NE

"...my wife has become my mother. I don't know when this happened, but I noticed it recently when she called my office and asked what I'd eaten for lunch, then asked what time I'd be home, and reminded me to button up because of the windchill."

—CLARKE, KALAMAZOO, MI

"...when she's tense, she tears paper. I find little pieces of tissues and paper napkins all over the floor. At a family reunion, she shredded an entire tablecloth."

—DAVID, CASPER, WY

"...she can't relax. Relaxing makes her nervous. She worries about it, feels guilty, as if she *should* be using her time to do something useful or productive. She feels wrong if she even has the *opportunity* to relax."

—FELIX, TOLEDO, OH

"...if a black cat crosses the road, she'll drive around the block so it won't cross her path. There are no salt shakers on our table so no one will spill salt. She won't let our daughters take the last serving of any food, for fear they'll be old maids. Yet she's furious if I imply that she's superstitious."

—ANDY, RICHMOND, VA

"...she believes in spirits. She won't have an antique in the house unless she knows about and approves of the people it belonged to."

—PETER, LARCHMONT, NY

"I LOVE HER, BUT..."

"...she cannot keep a secret. The very idea of secrecy makes her so nervous that she spills the beans. Her brother is coming to town to surprise their sister for her fortieth birthday. My wife has managed, so far, not to tell her sister that he's coming. She has, however, asked her sister where he should stay."

—TONY, EUREKA, NV

"...she anthropomorphizes everything. Our cars. The coffeemaker. The micro-wave. The computer. They all have names, feelings, moods and opinions."

—VINCE, HOPE, NM

"...she corrects my grammar."

—NICK, PHILADELPHIA, PA

"I LOVE HER, BUT..."

"...she uses trendy buzzwords. She 'relates' to this or that. She 'shares' thoughts. Oh, and she loves lots of syllables. It's an 'establishment,' never a 'place.' Or 'edifice' instead of 'building.' If she can't find a word that sounds impressive, she makes one up. Systemization. Reductionship. Impactification."

—JULIUS, CLEVELAND, OH

"...her 'S's whistle. Sometimes this gets to me."

—HERB, MADISON, WI

"...she can't abide silence. She'll say *anything* to fill a gap. If she's awake, she's talking."

—GEORGE, ARLINGTON, VA

"...she's too honest. Even if she struggles to keep her mouth shut, her face gives her away. She'll stare right at people, with her mouth open. Or she'll laugh out loud at them when they don't intend to be funny."

—GUY, CORPUS CHRISTI, TX

"... she interrupts herself, never finishes a sentence. Stops right in the middle and starts on another topic. You have to ask her to finish what she was saying, and half the time she doesn't remember, or she looks at you like what's the matter with you that you need everything spelled out? Why can't you just understand?"

—SAL, BINGHAMTON, NY

"...she talks in pronouns. This, they, those, them, it, he. I have to ask her which 'they' or what 'this,' because she never gives the antecedent."

—DAN, FORT WASHINGTON, PA

"...everything's the absolute 'best' or 'worst.' There's no middle ground."

—RUSS, LAKE GENEVA, WI

"...she has a cliché for every occasion.
'That's the way the cookie crumbles.'
Or, 'You can't cry over spilt milk.'"

—LEON, WASHINGTON, DC

"...she whispers—when she talks you have to lean over and put your ear next to her mouth, or you can't hear what she's saying. She complains that I'm hard of hearing."

—ETHAN, RICHMOND, VA

"I LOVE HER, BUT..."

"...she's the one who tells the bride that her bra strap's been showing during the ceremony. Or who passes her dinner entrée to me, explaining to our hostess that I'll eat *anything*. Or who remarks to a friend that the added pounds look *good*; they take away some of the wrinkles."

—BILL, NEW YORK, NY

"…whenever I'm leaving the room, she decides to talk to me. She's always got one more thing to say. So now, instead of actually leaving, I stand outside the door and wait till the count of three, and, sure enough, she calls, 'Donny—'"

—DON, LOS ANGELES, CA

"...I'm married to Mrs. Malaprop. She mixes metaphors, makes Freudian slips. She told the neighborhood bully to stop 'imitating' the other kids. I told her the word she wanted was 'intimidate.' She said, 'Warren, these kids are only seven years old! They aren't thinking about sex!'"

—WARREN, FORT WAYNE, IN

"...if there's a mirror around, she's in it. She poses. Puckers, practices batting her eyes."

—DOUG, NEW ORLEANS, LA

"...she's *always* on the phone. I put in an extra line, so I can make a call now and then. But when I pick it up, she's got somebody on hold."

—SAM, BRONX, NY

"...whenever we go anywhere, she wants us to dress alike, in the same colors, even matching shirts and slacks. Like twins."

—LARRY, ATLANTA, GA

"...she will not wear her glasses. People must think she's a snob, but she's not ignoring them; she just doesn't see anything. She has no idea who's standing next to her. Hell, sometimes her shoes don't match."

—DANIEL, BALTIMORE, MD

"... she wears these false eyelashes. She left 'em lying around and I slammed 'em with my newspaper, tried to kill the damn things. Scared me half to death."

—GORDON, OKLAHOMA CITY, OK

"...every so often, she studies fashion magazines and decides to change her style, make herself over with a whole new image. She buys all new clothes, gets her hair restyled, maybe changes the color. Costs me a fortune. And a few months later, she decides she'll change everything back."

—MEL, CHICAGO, IL

"I LOVE HER, BUT..."

"...my wife doesn't function well without a lot of accessories."

—JOHN, NEW YORK, NY

"...her purse weighs more than she does. Whatever you need, it's in there: bandaids, aspirin, chewing gum, a toothbrush kit, matches, probably a couple hand grenades. But she can never find a credit card, a dollar bill or a tissue. This doesn't bother her, though. Searching her purse is an ongoing life process."

—SCOTT, HINGHAM, MA

"...wherever she is, she takes her shoes off. In the theater, at a restaurant, in her office. Once, we had four rows of an airplane searching so we could get ready to disembark."

—NATE, GOLD HILL, CO

"...there is absolutely no order to what she does. Her path is zigzags and circles. She gets dressed and *then* decides to take a shower. She comes home from the grocery with eggs and *then* decides that we need bread, too. This is not annoying to her. It's just how she operates."

—ADAM, PENNINGTON, NJ

"...she *never* does just one thing at a time. She's mopping the floor, doing squats, cooking soup, talking on the phone to a client, baking and doing laundry all at once. She's like a windup toy gone mad. Even when we have sex, I suspect that she's planning her next sales presentation or tomorrow's grocery list."

—TIM, WYNNEWOOD, PA

"...she analyzes every angle of every situation. She can't make a decision without discussing 'on the other hand,' the decision's implications, possible outcomes, possible repercussions and alternatives. It can take an hour to decide which dress to wear to a meeting, or what meal to order in a restaurant. Then she has to tell me, step by step, how she arrived at her decision."

—MORT, MINNEAPOLIS, MN

"…my wife has no sense of direction. The kids are only five and six, but they know the score. 'Oh, no,' they say. 'Mommy's driving.' And they ask to take snacks."

—ARNIE, SUNAPEE, NH

"...she gestures while she talks. Even while she's driving. If you sit too close, you can get bopped in the eye."

—GERALD, MILLER, IN

"...to her, green means go yellow means go faster, red means slow down enough to see if a cop's around, then floor it."

—MICHAEL, AUSTIN, TX

"... If someone tries to pass her, she speeds up. She cuts people off, bares her teeth, curses, flashes the finger at other drivers. All her aggressions come out behind the wheel."

—DARNELL, CHRISTMAS COVE, ME

"... when I'm driving, she reaches over and turns on the window washer because *she* can't see. Or, if it's drizzling, she turns on the wipers, which smear the water on the window; if I complain about the smears, she puts the washer on so the window's all splashed and I can't see at all."

—NED, MANCHESTER, NH

"…she will not use the self-service gas line, won't pump her own. She'd rather run out of gas."

—JON, EVANSTON, IL

"...she finds meaning in every interaction, no matter how minuscule. Every gesture, handshake or word. Where people sit or stand in a room. After a party, she'll say, 'What do you think he meant by the look he gave her when she sat next to his wife?' Nothing's too minute for analysis."

—ROBERT, PINE BLUFF, AR

"...you'd think she knew every Hollywood celebrity personally, the way she talks. She gossips about them, about who's cheating, who's splitting up, who's had a boob job, who's making how many millions."

—TOM, TOLEDO, OH

"...she takes those soaps too seriously. I'll come home and find her in tears because some character died. Or upset that some nonexistent guy's having a fictional affair."

—ARCHIE, ST. LOUIS, MO

"...she puts on airs. When she answers the phone, 'Hello' is a five-syllable word."

—PATRICK, NANTUCKET, MA

"...she ought to be a spy. The woman can get anyone to tell her anything. At the company picnic, I bet her she couldn't get the story on the CEO's new wife. Five minutes later she comes back, says, 'Twenty-seven, has an MBA and she's four months pregnant.' Strangers in doctors' offices, airports, wherever she is, people tell her their life stories."

—STEVE, HOUSTON, TX

"I LOVE HER, BUT..."

"...my wife's sure that every woman we know is after me. At least, every blonde. It's flattering but, unfortunately, not true."

—KYLE, TULSA, OK

"I LOVE HER, BUT..."

"...she's a chameleon. Becomes just like whomever she's around. Conservatives or liberals, pro-Choice or pro-Life. I've heard her accent change within seconds to Southern, British, Russian or Brooklyn. She says the way to draw people out is to make them feel as if they're among their own kind. But who knows who she really is?"

—WAYNE, WASHINGTON, DC

"...she never lets a subject drop. People turn to dust while she clings to a topic."

—ZACH, PEORIA, IL

"...she relies completely on her intuition. You can't argue or reason her out of her impressions. She sees no need to back up her opinions with evidence or facts. Her gut feelings are all that matter."

—BOB, DES MOINES, IA

"I LOVE HER, BUT..."

"... she cries easily. Happy things, sad things, future things, past things. Things that haven't happened. Things that might. News stories. TV commercials. A flower. A loose tooth."

—MACE, MARBLEHEAD, MA

"...when she's depressed or had a bad day at the office, she drowns her sorrows in chocolate. A double hot fudge sundae, or devil's food mocha cake. But she won't have a drink with me. Too many calories."

—DAVE, BETHESDA, MD

"...she worries about things that she can't *do* anything about. Whatever she reads in the newspaper. Ebola, hurricanes, melanoma, interest rates, ozone, crime, whales."

—AL, DALLAS, TX

"...everything's a problem. Or a potential problem. She sees every situation in terms of what might be wrong or go wrong and plans for the 'worst case.'"

—DREW, TALLAHASSEE, FL

"…if she can't find anything else to worry about, she'll worry that she worries too much."

—CHRIS, PALO ALTO, CA

"...she's a capable, professional woman and she can't stand it if anyone talks down to her. But she reserves the right to play dumb when she wants to. She's talked her way out of a hundred traffic tickets by batting those lashes and cooing, 'I'm sorry, Officer, I didn't see that little old light.' And she manipulates me the same way. It works every time."

—DREW, JACKSON, MS

"I LOVE HER, BUT…."

"…she can ruin any joke. She'll include the punchline in the setup. Or get a critical fact wrong. Or go off on a tangent. Like she'll tell you why the salesman was on the road and what his product line was and how he got along with his boss before she ever remembers to tell you that, oh, by the way, he met this farmer's daughter."

—GUY, CORPUS CHRISTI, TX

"...she never gets an off-color joke. I have to explain."

—MAC, EVANSTON, IL

"...she praises people in a way that causes a stir. Let's see. She made a fuss over my sister, told her how much guts she has to defy fashion and wear such 'comfortable' shoes. Oh. And she praised my nephew for choosing a bride for her character rather than something superficial like good looks."

—DEL, DALLAS, TX

"...when she changes her mind, she expects me somehow to know, automatically, without being told. This doesn't matter so much when it's about whether to buy waxed or unwaxed dental floss. But it can also be about what time or place we were supposed to meet for dinner."

—IAN, BUFFALO, NY

"...to her, everything's black or white; there are no shades of gray. Everything's either right or wrong, good or evil, and if you're in doubt about which is which, just ask her."

—DEAN, LOUISVILLE, KY

"...the woman can't make up her mind. About anything. Ever. When she finally appears to have made a decision, you can bet your life that in a minute, you'll hear, 'Actually, I changed my mind...'"

—WILL, WINSTON-SALEM, NC

"...she'll decide to go to a movie when it's too late to get there. She waits till the registration deadline passes to decide to take a class. She registered to vote two days after the last election."

—MARTY, BOSTON, MA

"...she forgets what she's told whom, and she gets caught. Like when she claimed that her apricot pecan torte was a famous family tradition to the woman who gave her the recipe."

—MITCH, BATON ROUGE, LA

"...she will not give out a recipe; she pretends not to remember it. She never reveals the names of our cleaning help or baby-sitters. She nearly killed me when I gave our neighbor the name of our kids' piano teacher."

—HIRAM, HARTFORD, CT

"... if there's a rumor going around, she'll know about it. Hell. She probably *started* it."

—RUSSELL, HONOLULU, HI

"...she gets so excited about Christmas, she tells everyone what their presents are before they're opened."

—KEN, FRAMINGHAM, MA

"... when we eat out, she orders in 'French.' Even French-speaking waiters can't understand her."

—WAYNE, SOUTHFIELD, MI

"...she's creative with finances. If she buys a pair of shoes or a dress on sale, she'll say: 'I saved you forty dollars today. Why don't we split it— Give me twenty bucks.'"

—SAM, NORTHBROOK, IL

THE CASH CLASH

Men get an apparent charge out of complaining about their wives' spending habits. With laughter and curses, they describe mall predators, bargain scavengers, plastic melters and kitsch collectors. Whether they're spenders or savers, couples inevitably clash about their cash, credit, assets and debits.

Husbands declare that their wives use cents without sense, see money as a commodity of autonomy not economy, spend primarily to impress others or express themselves. "Interest, to her," one man laments, "is what she has in clothes."

Whatever their specific gripes, however, most men claim that they can bank on the consistency of their wives' financial behavior. "It's no use trying to change her," one husband concludes. "I might as well save my breath. And, married to her, that's probably all I'll ever save."

"...small countries survive for a year on less money than my wife spends in a month at the beauty parlor."

—MIKE, NASHVILLE, TN

"... she insists on cutting my
hair. This is her idea of saving
money."

—PHILIP, BETHESDA, MD

"...her system for economizing is to charge everything. That way, she doesn't have to pay. Cash never touches her hands."

—DAVE, BOSTON, MA

"...she spends hours clipping coupons to save three or four dollars at the supermarket, but spends hours running up bills on the car phone. She buys generic cold medicines, but uses the full-service gas line. She can't see a problem with this."

—MARK, CLEVELAND, OH

"...her idea of what to do when a button falls off is to buy a new shirt. If a battery dies, you replace the car. It never occurs to her to fix anything."

—DON, LOS ANGELES, CA

"...she scours thrift shops.
Buys me some dead guy's ties.
Or sweaters somebody else
has thrown away."

—JACK, BALTIMORE, MD

"...when we go bowling or out to eat, whatever we do for 'fun,' she complains that we're blowing our money. We should save it for the kids' college or our retirement. But it doesn't stop her from planning the next outing."

—DOUG, NEWARK, NJ

"...she balances the checkbook. Well, to the nearest hundred dollars."

—NORM, SKOKIE, IL

"...she never—and I mean *never*—records checks."

—HANK, RICHMOND, VA

"...she insists on balancing the checkbook to the penny.
No matter how long it takes."

—JIM, TUCSON, AZ

"I LOVE HER, BUT..."

"...she balances the checkbook in her *head*. The woman estimates our grocery bill within a dime. Or our vacation expenses to the dollar. Even our taxes. This annoys me. I need a calculator to figure out *tips*."

—CHARLES, DES MOINES, IA

"...she's too good-hearted. She sends ten bucks to every charity that asks us for money. She takes down 800 numbers from the television, regardless of the cause, calls, then sends them checks. Of course, her generosity ensures that our name gets on more and more mailing lists asking for money, which means that she'll write more and more checks."

—TED, DETROIT, MI

"...she saves boxes from big-name stores, then uses them to wrap Christmas gifts she buys at discount marts."

—SEBASTIAN, ST. PAUL, MN

"...she only buys brand names. Status labels. This is true for cars, clothes, ketchup. Everything."

—LUKE, NAPLES, FL

"...if she sees a 'reduced' sign, she buys a hundred things we'll never need or use. Then she brags about how much money she's saved. 'I got forty per-cent off! You can't do better than that!'"

—JIM, MINNEAPOLIS, MN

"...now that she's working part-time, she justifies buying anything she wants. I'd estimate that, by Tuesday, she's spent her weekly paycheck about three times over."

—MILES, SHREVEPORT, LA

"...shopping is her life. Salespeople know her. She knows prices, sales dates, salespeople's days off. Their middle names. Their birthdays. Their shoe sizes."

—CARL, SEATTLE, WA

"...she insists on paying bills the day they arrive. The *minute* they arrive."

—BERNIE, DETROIT, MI

"I LOVE HER, BUT..."

"...she asks me what I like and then she buys my clothes and pays no attention whatsoever to my taste. I ask for plain light blue shirts, navy sweaters. I get floral jungle prints or patterns with animal faces woven into them."

—SCOT, ROCHESTER, NY

"... she orders all our clothes from catalogs to 'save time.' Then things don't fit. Or the colors are wrong. So she sends them back and orders other stuff. I spend more on postage than I do on the clothes."

—BERT, PORTLAND, ME

"...she hates to shop. Hates malls. Hates supermarkets. She says they're monuments to decadence and consumerism and she'd rather wear rags than go there. Which means that I have to go."

—BRUCE, DENVER, CO

"...she won't go to the supermarket until the refrigerator is absolutely empty. She won't throw out a leftover until it crawls. Even then, she's likely to think of a way to cook it to death or disguise it with sauce. Waste not, want not."

—TYRONE, JACKSON HOLE, WY

"...she will not shop at discount stores or sales. She thinks they're crowded and plebeian. She doesn't even look at the reduced rack, other than, perhaps, for gifts for my mother."

—CONRAD, WILMINGTON, DE

"...she shops on impulse. I'll come home and a grand piano will be in the living room, a satellite dish on the roof."

—DENNIS, BETHESDA, MD

"...all she talks about is how much so-and-so is 'worth.' Who married money. Who earns what. Who bought what. Who's behind in their mortgage payments."

—DAVE, ST. LOUIS, MO

"...she doesn't part easily with a penny. She gets upset for days if her friends split their lunch check evenly, when all she had was a salad. She paid, maybe, two dollars more than her share. Not counting the *tip*!"

—WILL, ATLANTA, GA

"...she insists on carrying twenty dollars clipped to her underwear. For what purpose? Ah. For 'emergencies.' Okay. There she is in an emergency. What's she going to do, undress right where she is?"

—NICK, AUSTIN, TX

"...she never has any money, has no idea where it goes. No matter how much she earns or how much I give her, she's always flat broke."

—MIKE, KANSAS CITY, MO

"...she never looks at price tags."

—MONTE, WESTPORT, CT

"...she buys me gifts. And she has great taste. The sky's the limit. No problem. After all, I get the bills."

—ROGER, LOS ANGELES, CA

"...if *she's* cold, she makes kids wear sweaters. If *she's* tired, she sends them to bed."

—BILL, ALLENTOWN, PA

KIDS...

Room for Daddy

Husbands are no longer just bread-winners and disciplinarians. These days, "Wait till your father gets home" isn't necessarily a warning of impending punishment; more likely, it means that lunch-box-packing, storytelling, shoe-shopping, home-work-helping or bath-giving are temporarily delayed.

But, while some wives welcome Dad's participation, others are less than enthusiastic. Some couples find that, when the second parent becomes involved in daily rules and routines, opportunities for disagreement, disorganization and dysfunction double.

One man sums it up. "When I don't watch the kids, I catch it for not doing my part. When I do watch them, I catch it for not doing it right."

"...for almost thirty years, my wife has hung on to locks of hair from their first haircuts, and all their baby teeth, labeled in jars. She has their baby shoes, tagged by age and size. She has their spoons, bottles, toothbrushes, rattles, cuddly toys, blankets. Their pacifiers. She has Little League caps, Girl Scout and Boy Scout badges. Their games—Monopoly, Parcheesi, checkers. Their schoolwork, through high school. She keeps all of it, neatly organized and marked. If they ever have second childhoods, she's stocked."

—LEW, FRAMINGHAM, MA

"...she lets them answer the phone. She thinks it's 'cute.' When I call from the office to talk to her, they chat with me and then hang up. I can't get through to her."

—CLAY, WILMINGTON, DE

"...it annoys her that our children look like me."

—JAMES, NEW ORLEANS, LA

"...counting my wife and our teenage girls, that's four women. Somebody's *always* got PMS."

—EVERETT, LITTLE ROCK, AR

"...she asks them about their bowel movements. Every day. She says that her grandmother asked her mother and her mother asked her. And she adds, 'At least I don't make them keep a chart.'"

—DWIGHT, CHEVY CHASE, MD

"...she lets them fix their own breakfasts so they'll 'learn.' And there have been some true learning experiences. I still can smell eggs burning in the toaster oven. And then there was the time they tried to make breakfast shakes, putting bananas and peaches in the blender. With the pits."

—DIGGER, GREELEY, CO

"...she lets the kids eat her food right off her plate. And so she never has a meal. She munches what they leave."

—TONY, MEDFORD, NJ

"...she makes the boys eat lima beans. Hell. *I* don't eat lima beans!"

—GENE, GRAND RAPIDS, MI

"...she treats kids like plants. She feeds them, gives them lots of fresh air and sunshine, and lets nature do the rest."

—GIL, BOISE, ID

"...she's big on health foods and home remedies. Lots of herbs and teas. Sees herself as a medicine woman."

—BERT, SANTE FE, NM

"...she nursed each child forever. The youngest was four when she finally stopped. I thought it was enough when they were old enough to unbutton her blouse themselves."

—DYLAN, WILMINGTON, DE

"...she's always sniffing them. Their clothes. Their breath. Their hands. Their hair. Their feet."

—BEN, MEMPHIS, TN

"...you don't want to go in the bathroom after she gives them a bath. The walls and the ceiling are soaked, toys are everywhere and you're sliding, up to your ankles in bubbles."

—BOBBY, SPOKANE, WA

"...her idea of table manners is to tell our three-year-old to keep her food on her plate and not to put her feet on the table. At least not while we're eating."

—MIKE, ST. LOUIS, MO

"... when the kids get out of line, she says, 'They take after your father. They have your genes. They didn't get that from my side.'"

—DICK, TACOMA, WA

"...for fun, she has screaming contests with the kids. They see who can get to the highest, loudest pitch. She thinks it's healthy, fun, tension-relieving. Sooner or later, someone's gonna call the cops. Probably me."

—IAN, BOULDER, CO

"...she gets too close with our sons' girlfriends. When they break up, she misses them. Mopes and mourns for weeks at a time."

—EARL, SAN JOSE, CA

"...she bats her eyes at our daughter's dates."

—JIM, FORT LAUDERDALE, FL

"...she does whatever the kids do. Roller-blade, skate board, body surf, climb trees, catch caterpillars. I hope this stops when they start dating."

—NELSON, SAN FRANCISCO, CA

"...when our son gets a pimple, she chases him around the house till he lets her squeeze it."

—BOB, GLENVIEW, IL

"...whenever she doesn't want to deal with something, she says, 'Go ask your father.'"

—BRAD, SOMERSET, NJ

"...she makes them perform for company. Sing or play their piano songs. Not just one or two numbers, but a whole entire concert. People roll their eyes and squirm. She beams with pride."

—EDGAR, ST. PAUL, MN

"I LOVE HER, BUT..."

"...she hangs their 'artwork' all over the house. Every room's decorated with houses, rainbows and unidentified colored objects. She raves about their work as if they were baby Picassos. Our five-year-old recently confided, 'Dad, don't tell Mom, but *some* of my pictures are just scribble-scrabble.'"

—JULES, RALEIGH, N.C.

"...she wanted to be in a rock band. So we've got a drummer, a sax player and two electric guitarists. Amplifiers and everything."

—JOEL, WICHITA, KS

"...structure's primo to her. No deviations. Rules are rules. Bedtime's at eight, tired or not. Bathtime's at seven, dirty or not. Dinner's at six, hungry or not. That's how it is, like it or not."

—GEORGE, TOLEDO, OH

"...she thinks it's good for the children to see her win our arguments. This, she says, will make her a strong role model for our daughters, and make our son a more enlightened husband."

—KEVIN, ANCHORAGE, AK

"...she encourages them to negotiate, rather than to obey. If I say it's time for bed, I've got two little girls trying to make a better deal. If I give them an allowance, they try to bargain for a raise. I never hear, 'Yes, Dad.' I hear, 'Dad, that *can't* be your best offer.'"

—JEROME, LOUISVILLE, KY

"...she buys the kids every toy, game or outfit she ever wanted."

—ZACH, GLENVIEW, IL

"...she makes lists of what skills the twins should have. Not just for now, while they're in preschool. We're talking for life. Reading lists. Art classes. Violin lessons. College."

—GERALD, AMHERST, MA

"...wherever they go, she dresses them to 'represent the family.' They can't look scruffy or grubby or have mussed-up hair. And Lord help them if they have dirt under their nails."

—MONTE, CHESTER, CT

"I LOVE HER, BUT..."

"...we haven't got our own, so she mothers everyone at her office. She knows their personal lives, calls them at home, and they call here at all hours. There's no border between home and work. And she can never fire anyone; they're her kids."

—PETE, CHERRY HILL, NJ

"...the dog is her baby. She lets him eat off her plate, kisses his mouth."

—ELLIOT, PITTSBURGH, PA

"…There are no absolutes in our home. To her, rules are made to be broken, or at least bent."

—JEREMY, MIAMI, FL

"...she's forever handing me a camera and telling me to— quick—get that picture. Then she yells at me for missing the shot. Whatever it was."

—PRESTON, PORTLAND, OR

"...the television's her after-school baby-sitter. The kids are dazed, glued. And when they're not watching, they're singing the jingles from Nickelodeon, acting out scenes from reruns of *Full House*."

—WALLACE, HUNTINGDON VALLEY, PA

"...our car's full of half-eaten kids' snacks, spare diapers, books, markers, sticky patches, toys, half-eaten lollipops, shoes, clothes, half-empty juice boxes. I get in clean and pressed, and get dropped at the train station looking like a refugee escaping the play group from Hell."

—BEAR, GILLETTE, WY

"... she lets the kids interrupt. We can't ever have a conversation. Or anything else."

—MIKE, NEW ORLEANS, LA

"...with five kids, I don't have time to complain about my wife. I don't have time to notice her."

—BOB, CHARLESTON, WV

"... she buys books on child-rearing and leaves them for me to read. Or she outlines the major points and faxes her notes to my office."

—KEITH, MADISON, WI

"...she doesn't want to go *anywhere* without the kids. 'What if we get killed in a car accident? What if the plane crashes?' If she had her way, the whole family'd be joined together at the hip."

—TONY, JACKSON, MS

"...she lets the kids fall asleep in our bed so they'll feel 'secure.' There's little arms and legs squirming and tossing all over the place. If I want to sleep, I go to one of the kids' beds."

—PHIL, SAN DIEGO, CA

"I LOVE HER, BUT..."

"…every time I turn around, there's a new animal in the house. They find a garden snake. Their mom says, of course, they can keep it. Their rooms sound like a jungle and smell like a zoo. They've got the snake, gerbils, fish, a dog, a parrot. That I know of."

—WAYNE, TOLEDO, OH

"I LOVE HER, BUT..."

"... she thinks teens should make their own decisions. If they don't want to study, shower, get up in the morning or eat with the family, that's up to them. She tells me not to order them around, that'll only make things worse. She says the consequences of their actions will be their best teachers. But she protects them and sees to it that there are no consequences."

—ZACH, PORTSMOUTH, NH

"...she embarrasses the kids all the time. She still kisses the boys goodbye everyday at the bus stop even though they're in high school."

—PRESTON, PORTLAND, OR

"...she invites people over without telling me about it. I'm hanging out in my jockey shorts, vegging, and three couples I've never seen before show up for a barbecue."

—DOM, BUFFALO, NY

SIDE BY SIDE

Just as one man's heaven is another's hell, rapture for one spouse can be torture for the other. Although most husbands agree that fun, whatever its form, is essential to a successful marriage, they also warn that forcing partners to participate in pet projects can be dangerous.

"I don't take my wife pheasant hunting," one husband says. "And she doesn't make me play bridge."

Even if some of their favorite activities are

best enjoyed sans mates, there are others that require companionship. Couples find fun that's as simple as staying home, as complicated as computer games, as dangerous as skydiving, as mundane as walking the malls.

And even when their wives' preferences take precedence, most men cope well with it. "It doesn't matter what we do," one romantic said. "We're stuck with each other. So we might as well party."

"...one of her great pleasures is mimicking my mother. Actually, she's not bad at it."

—AL, DALLAS, TX

"I LOVE HER, BUT..."

"...she has a big family, and she loves to have them around. Some brother or cousin's always over, his head in the fridge, making a sandwich, eating the piece of pie I was saving, helping himself to my best Scotch. Or their wives are there, borrowing clothes for their kids, which they never return."

—VINNY, BROOKLYN, NY

"...whenever we visit somebody, she brings her own food, in case she doesn't like what they're serving. Then she tells people she's on a special diet."

—CARL, MEMPHIS, TN

"...she's out of control. Once, at a party, she meant to say, 'Sorry we're late; we got lost.' But what she said was, 'Sorry we're late; we got laid.' Then she realized what she'd said and laughed so hard she wet her pants. At a wedding, she commented aloud, 'The bride and her sisters all look just like Minnie Mouse. How can he tell which one he's marrying?'"

—MIKE, RALEIGH, NC

"...she's phobic about mold and fungus. She will not look inside an open sour cream container, or a half-used package of cream cheese."

—LANCE, ASPEN, CO

"...she listens to Barry Manilow."

—STU, GLENCOE, IL

"...she loves Country. Wails along with it. Wants me to go line-dancing with her."

—WALTER, DARIEN, CT

"...she takes singing lessons. She has the voice of a scalded cat. I had no idea what that sound was when I first heard it. She refers to her body as her 'instrument.'"

—BRAD, MINNEAPOLIS, MN

"... she can't stand cartoons. Even *Bullwinkle*."

—ROBIN, GLADWYNE, PA

"...when she plays Scrabble, her personality changes. She becomes vicious, relentless, bloodthirsty. She has no pity. Will do anything to win."

—DEXTER, GRAND RAPIDS, MI

"...she loves gold, wears lots of chains and bangles. She makes quite a jangle when she moves. Can hardly lift her arm."

—JASON, LOS ANGELES, CA

"...she counts my beers."

—ZEKE, OCONOMOWOC, WI

"I LOVE HER, BUT..."

"...for some reason, she likes to read the labels on cans and boxes of food. Aloud."

—MORT, OMAHA, NE

"... she doesn't always tighten the lids when she puts jars away. I remember this a nanosecond before the pickles and glass hit the floor."

—WEBSTER, BUTTE, MT

"I LOVE HER, BUT..."

"...she can't say no so we have no time for ourselves. She's always doing favors for other people, the school or the church. People are always dropping by, she overbooks our weekends, volunteers for everything. Complains that we have no time for fun."

—DEL, DETROIT, MI

"…whenever somebody's dies or gets sick, she brings lasagna to their house. When you smell lasagna, you know something bad has happened."

—PATRICK, PITTSBURGH, PA

"...she hates winter. She's in a funk from October to April."

—OLIVER, OSHKOSH, WI

"...she enjoys nothing more than talking on the phone. She *does* nothing more than talk on the phone."

—GEORGE, CHARLOTTE, NC

"...chocolate. As far as I can tell, that's her greatest passion."

—DAVE, SAVANNAH, GA

"...she loves slasher movies.
That makes me nervous."

—JODY, JACKSON, MS

"...wherever she goes, even if it's for a couple of hours, she packs a snack. Like a survival kit. There's always a sandwich or some chocolate chips in her purse."

—RALPH, PROVIDENCE, RI

"... come hell or high water, she must go out every Saturday night. It doesn't matter where or with whom. She'd rather eat out in some greasy spoon or go to a bad movie with a couple she despises than stay at home."

—DAN, BUFFALO, NY

"...she must have a gift to give wherever she goes, or she won't go. She can't arrive 'empty-handed' anywhere. Even a business meeting. Or a funeral."

—JB, ERIE, PA

"I LOVE HER, BUT..."

"...at restaurants or parties, when ever there's an opportunity, she eavesdrops. She'd much rather listen in on other people than have our own conversation. The whole way home, she talks about what she's heard."

—ROB, RENO, NV

"...she's always late. It's bad enough when we're visiting other people. But it's worse when *our* guests show up and she hasn't even showered, and greets them in sweaty workout clothes. They wait and I serve drinks while she bathes and does her hair. By the time she's dressed and made up, everyone's half in the bag."

—ED, NAPLES, FL

"I LOVE HER, BUT..."

"...she insists on arriving fashionably late. Once we were so fashionable that we got to the party after the guests had all left. The host answered the door in his pajamas. This had no effect on her; she still wants to be the last one to arrive."

—TERRY, NEW HAVEN, CT

"...after every social event, she needs instant analysis. What each person probably thought of her, if she said the right things, how she looked. We have to rehash every one of her interactions."

—JEFF, SCARSDALE, NY

"...she never tells me we're going somewhere until it's time to dress."

—ARCHIE, PITTSBURGH, PA

"...she gives me a surprise birthday party every year. The biggest birthday surprise would be no surprise party."

—DEX, BOULDER, CO

"...she overpacks. Big-time."

—GORDON, PORTLAND, ME

"...when we travel, she brings a can of Lysol to sterilize the hotel toilet seats and telephones."

—JON, NEW ORLEANS, LA

"I LOVE HER, BUT..."

"...out of the blue, she'll say, 'I'd like to run naked around the South Pole.' Or, 'I want to spend time with people who live with yaks.' Her mind's always someplace else. On a bike trip through the Alps or parachuting into the Amazon. She thinks I'm a wimp because I like to go places that have room service."

—LARRY, SAN JOSE, CA

"...she's jealous of my boat. She denies this, but I know she is."

—ANGELO, SARASOTA, FL

"...she goes fishing with me, but then talks about how sorry she is for all the cute little fish."

—HERB, NORTHEAST, MD

"... she likes to shoot. Any kind of gun. And she's a good shot, too. She goes through boxes of ammo, says shooting relaxes her, takes the knots out of her neck. Scares the hell out of me!"

—BRAM, KNOXVILLE, TN

"I LOVE HER, BUT..."

"...she's a do-it-yourselfer. She snakes the toilet. Prunes the bushes. Browses the hardware stores. I dare not point out the bubbles in the wallpaper or the bristlemarks in the paint. She's usually holding a hammer."

—JIM, MINNEAPOLIS, MN

"...she's always redecorating. Always changing things around. Moving furniture. Nothing's where it was. I have to be careful when I leave the room for a minute, or I can come back and plop into a chair that isn't there anymore."

—TRAVIS, BISMARCK, ND

"...she kills every plant she comes close to. But she won't give up, loves to 'garden.'"

—HARRY, KNOXVILLE, TN

"...everything's a contest. How late we work, how much we earn, how much weight we lose, how many books we read, how fast we read them. I've learned not to win."

—WAYNE, STAMFORD, CT

"...she loves gossip. Nothing pleases her as much as a juicy rumor."

—ROY, FORT WORTH, TX

"...when we play tennis, she gives me running commentary. 'Stand there. Follow through. Bend your knees! Aw, Pete, you shoulda had that.'"

—PETE, WILMINGTON, DE

"...she's always on the Internet, chatting. I can go out and come back, and she doesn't even know I was gone."

—MITCH, SAN FRANCISCO, CA

"I LOVE HER, BUT..."

"...her favorite thing is to have her feet rubbed. She plops them into my lap, and they stay there, waiting and wiggling until they get what they want."

—MAURICE, AMES, IA

"...she has too much fun. She plays tennis, gets her nails done, her hair done. Shops. Goes out to lunch. Pays the maid, orders new sofas. Plays with the kids. She's got it made. If there's reincarnation, next life, I'm coming back as my wife."

—MARC, GLADWYNE, PA

"...when she's mad or upset, she plays this old Simon and Garfunkel song over and over and over. 'Bridge over Troubled Waters.' It's a nice song, but after two or three hours of it, I'll apologize, promise whatever, say anything, just to get her to stop playing it."

—SETH, ST. CLOUD, MN

LOVE AND WAR...

KEEPING THE PEACE

At times, conflicts occur in even the happiest of homes. And, when it comes to fighting, many men claim that women are definitely the unfairer sex. Some seasoned husbands say they've given up trying to win; rather, they strive to lose as little as possible, yielding minimum ground.

Whether the issues are ongoing or intermittent, silent or shouted, some husbands find their mates to be illogical, unpredictable, inconsistent, obtuse, transparent, frustrating or flighty. No matter what the content of their particular arguments, even the toughest, most macho husbands agree that a surrender, disguised as a negotiated settlement, is usually the wisest course.

"There's no battle fatigue worse," a retired Marine declares, "than that from girlilla warfare."

"...she never apologizes.

Never."

—TOM, ST. LOUIS, MO

"...right and wrong are unimportant to her. Reason and logic are irrelevant. How she *feels* is all that matters. A fight isn't over until she 'feels' okay again."

—MATT, RANDOLPH, VT

"...when we got married, we agreed not to go to bed mad. To her, that means either *I* give in and apologize or we stay up all night fighting. There's no third option."

—RICK, CORPUS CHRISTI, TX

"...when she's mad, she looks me up and down like I just got out of a spacecraft. Like I'm the dumbest, most absurd creature she's ever laid eyes on."

—STU, KENOSHA, WI

"...she's never wrong. Never has been, never will be."

—BILL, SAN JOSE, CA

"I LOVE HER, BUT..."

"...she won't let me get a word in. She talks while I talk, right on top of my words. She never listens to what I'm saying, answers what she *thinks* I'm going to say before I've had a chance not to say it."

—ED, SANTE FE, NM

"...she doesn't give a damn who's right. Even if I'm right beyond the shadow of a doubt, I have to be the one to apologize. She gives me the silent treatment. This wouldn't be so bad, except there's a great deal of door-slamming that goes with it."

—HOWARD, SKOKIE, IL

"...nothing makes her angrier than when she wants to argue and I say, 'You're right. I apologize.' Or, 'Yes, dear. I won't do it again.'"

—WARREN, NEW YORK, NY

"... when she's mad, her nostrils puff out and flare, and she sticks her chin up in the air like a tough guy. I don't dare tell her, but she looks like Popeye."

—JIM, SEATTLE, WA

"...she says a fight's not over until the opponent concedes. And she *never* concedes."

—GEOFF, FRAMINGHAM, MA

"...style counts at least ninety-nine per cent. If she doesn't like my tone of voice, or 'the way' I say, 'You're right,' she won't talk to me. If she doesn't like 'the way' I give her a gift, she won't take it. 'The way' I do something is more important than the intention or content."

—GENE, LAKE GENEVA, WI

"...she is a master of the no-win situation. If I don't help with the laundry, I'm wrong, but if I do, I'm still wrong for how I sort it. I'm wrong if I don't pay attention to her, but I'm piddling away money if I bring her flowers. She'll ask me to help make dinner, then she'll sit on my lap. Finally she'll get up and angrily do what she's asked *me* to do, annoyed that I haven't done it while she was sitting on me."

—LARRY, SEATTLE, WA

"...she can't stand it if I disagree with her. She won't let a subject drop for days. Weeks. Actually, come to think of it, she can go years. She's still trying to change my mind about where we *should* have gone on our honeymoon."

—OLLIE, BEAVER DAM, WI

"...she has to have the last word. Even if the last word is just a reminder that I might as well stop arguing, since she's going to continue the argument until she has the last word anyway."

—GARTH, SACRAMENTO, CA

"I LOVE HER, BUT..."

"...when she's mad, she doesn't care who knows it. She'll have it out right in public, at a party, in front of the neighbors or anybody. With words that make your ears steam. Then, when I apologize and it's over, she's instantly sweet as pie, as if nothing ever happened."

—GIL, ALBANY, NY

"...she gets mad when I tease her sister. But never gives me any credit for all the times I *don't*."

—TROY, BILLINGS, MT

"...I can't make peace by telling her that I love her. She snaps back, 'Your feelings are your business. How you *treat* me is *mine.*'"

—WARREN, KANSAS CITY, KS

"...the woman cannot see any point of view except from the angle of why I'm wrong."

—LARRY, DENVER, CO

"...she sees *any* willingness to compromise as a sign of an opponent's weakness. So, if I offer a compromise, she regroups and goes for the kill."

—SEAN, FRESNO, CA

"...the tension hangs around until we have sex. And, depending on how mad she is, that can be a while."

—HANK, CLEVELAND, OH

"...when she's upset, she talks faster and faster and her voice gets higher and higher. You almost expect her to take off and fly away."

—JOSEPH, BURLINGTON, VT

"...when she's mad, she puts the TV on real loud so I can't concentrate on anything else. If I turn it down, she turns it up again. The TV becomes the focus, and we take off from there."

—WES, LAKE FOREST, IL

"I LOVE HER, BUT..."

"... we've agreed not to fight in front of the kids. So, when the kids walk in on an argument, she becomes sugary, syrupy, sarcastically sweet. Believe me, it's much harder to take than her anger."

—BOB, FORESTVILLE, MD

"...she only likes to fight in public, in a crowd. She enjoys having an audience and creates these unforgettable, highly dramatic scenes."

—ROBERT, WILMINGTON, DE

"...when she's mad, she slams. Dishes, drawers. Doors. She doesn't use words, she uses sound effects."

—CHET, SAN FRANCISCO, CA

"...she does the martyr thing. Scrubs, fixes, cooks, toils dramatically, like a saint. She could win an Emmy for her sighing alone. But it's self-defeating. Because my incentive is to wait until she's finished whatever she's doing—cleaning the bathroom, baking muffins—before I deal with whatever's on her mind."

—ROY, HOUSTON, TX

"...expressing anger assertively is not her best skill. She lets me know she's mad by ignoring me. Or, if she's *really* mad, she raises an eyebrow."

—ARCHIE, PITTSBURGH, PA

"...she cross-examines me. Discovering what I had for lunch can involve twenty or thirty questions."

—ED, NAPLES, FL

"...if she thinks something's on my mind, she won't let me alone. She keeps asking, 'What's on your mind?' If I say, 'Nothing,' she argues with me. 'Something is. I can tell.' As if she knows what I'm thinking better than I do. Usually, I end up making something up, just to satisfy her."

—DEXTER, GRAND RAPIDS, MI

"...if she's mad, she expects me to know why. I'm supposed to be able to read her mind. If I ask her what's wrong, she gives me a look that could fry an egg and says, '*You* know what's wrong.' If I insist that I don't, she says, 'Well, you *should*.'"

—JERRY, LOUISVILLE, KY

"...it makes her mad if I get sick or hurt. Once I was carving a turkey and cut my hand. She scolded, 'What did you do *that* for?'"

—BRUCE, DENVER, CO

"...she's nine years older than I am and blames all our conflicts on my immaturity."

—STEPHEN, CHEVY CHASE, MD

"...she can't stick to the subject. My wife
cannot debate a simple, single issue. She
rambles off and rehashes everything she's
ever been mad at me about, everything I've
ever done wrong. She seems to think that if
I've been wrong in the past, it proves that
I'm wrong now."

—PATRICK, BOSTON, MA

"...she has a great throwing arm.
So we buy only unbreakable
tumblers, shatterproof glasses."

—DOUG, NEW ORLEANS, LA

"I LOVE HER, BUT..."

"...we spend less time arguing than we used to. We both know the routine and just cut to the chase. We don't need the middle anymore. Our fights are abbreviated. Then they just stop. They end unresolved because, by now, we each know the other will never give in."

—NEIL, WHITTIER, CA

"...when she gets mad,
she shops. So I apologize
or go broke."

—CALEB, SALEM, MA

"I LOVE HER, BUT..."

"...the longer we're married, the less noise our fights make. All she has to do is look at me and I know what she's thinking. She doesn't have to say a word, but I know she's nagging me, and I know what about. Nobody's uttered a syllable, but we're off. Now, I understand what my father meant when he used to tell my mother, 'Don't look at me in that tone of voice.'"

—FRANK, MALVERN, PA